# Reading begins at home

PREPARING CHILDREN FOR READING BEFORE THEY GO TO SCHOOL

## Dorothy Butler    Marie Clay

American edition prepared with the assistance of
Bobbye S. Goldstein, Reading Specialist, New York Public Schools

## Heinemann Educational Books

### Exeter, New Hampshire

**Heinemann Educational Books Inc.**
4 Front Street, Exeter, New Hampshire 03833

LONDON   EDINBURGH   MELBOURNE   AUCKLAND
HONG KONG   SINGAPORE   KUALA LUMPUR   NEW DELHI
IBADAN   NAIROBI   JOHANNESBURG
KINGSTON   PORT OF SPAIN

ISBN 0 435 08201 9

**Library of Congress Cataloging in Publication Data**

Butler, Dorothy, 1925-
   Reading begins at home.

   "First U.S. edition"—T.P. verso
   Bibliography: p.
   1. Children—Books and reading. 2. Reading readiness.
I. Clay, Marie M. II. Goldstein, Bobbye S. III. Title
Z1037 A1 B88 1982        028.5        82-6172
ISBN 0-435-08201-9                    AACR2

The publishers would like to thank Peter Dent for all the illustrations that accompany the text, and Carolyn Jenks, Children's Librarian, Exeter Public Library, for her help in compiling the list of books for children. Cover photograph of Andrew Borden and Mark Balfe was taken by Exeter Photo.


Printed in the United States of America

# Contents

1   First thoughts                           5

2   At home                                  8

3   Books, books, books                     17

4   More direct instruction                 23

5   Parents' questions                      29

6   Books for parents and children          39

**Other books by Marie Clay**
Published by Heinemann Educational Books, Exeter, N.H.

**OBSERVING YOUNG READERS**
Selected Papers

**READING: THE PATTERNING OF COMPLEX BEHAVIOUR**

**THE EARLY DETECTION OF READING DIFFICULTIES**
A Diagnostic Survey with Recovery Procedures

**CONCEPTS ABOUT PRINT TESTS:**
Sand
Stones

**WHAT DID I WRITE?**

# 1 First thoughts

## Should I teach my preschooler to read?

No one seemed to ask this question twenty years ago; now almost everyone either asks it, or feels uneasy about not doing so.

Is it true that the earlier we start 'teaching' reading the earlier a child will become a fluent reader? Or that reading failure (today's concern) can be avoided by an earlier start?

Before we can discuss these questions we need an answer to a much more basic one.

## What do we mean by 'reading'?

If we are going to teach reading we need to be clear about what reading is.

A definition which seems to take account of all the things a person must do to read successfully is given in a recent book for parents. Reading, says the author '...is the transfer of meaning from one mind to another through the medium of written language'.

There is nothing simple about the way this 'transfer' is accomplished; but the more fluently a person reads, the simpler it looks. We are inclined to feel that there must be a way of teaching children to read, a formula if you like, which will give each one the same key to the puzzle. Once they have that key, we feel, they will be set on the right road.

We are accustomed to breaking tasks into small units, and we probably want to break reading material into its obvious physical parts. These are letters, words and sentences.

Sounding out the words, which then become sentences, seems the logical way to read. In fact, this may seem the *only* way to do it. But is it?

It may be useful at this point to think of the way in which the child learns to speak. No one actually 'teaches' their child, and yet, by three or four years of age, that child will have learned to produce the right sounds, organized in an extremely complex way, to express an almost infinite number of ideas.

The child does this expertly, without direct help from adults. Children are not just mimics. They create sentences to express their thoughts. It is surely sensible to look closely at the method they use. What units of speech do they produce first?

You may say that the baby first says sounds and then single words. But anyone who has handled an eighteen-months-old baby will know that when the baby says 'ball' this means a great deal more than a name for a toy. She may be making one of many possible statements: 'There's my ball' with a pleased smile, on finding it; 'My ball has run away down the hill!' with outstretched arm and concerned expression; 'No! I don't want to go to bed! I want to play with my ball!' struggling desperately as a parent lowers her into her crib!

All these meanings, and many more can be understood when this child uses the one word 'ball'. She means us to understand the rest of the sentence because she cannot say it. There is no doubt that she has the meaning in her mind.

## Messages not letters and words

The child who is starting to learn to read is *not* a baby; at four or five years of age he is using language well for speaking purposes. Isn't the 'single word' the correct approach for him? There is considerable evidence that the majority of 'failed' readers see reading as the task of saying the words aloud correctly, one after the other, and not as a process of 'getting the message'. On the other hand, young children who are becoming good readers can often be seen almost swallowing the print whole, keeping the sense going by a miraculous mobilization of all the resources at their disposal—an exhilarating experience!

This seems to suggest that paying attention to 'the message' is a helpful idea. Actually, children

have to master this sooner or later, regardless of how they start.

You may want to protest that letters and words are important in learning to read. Of course they are both of crucial importance. We all know that language cannot be written down without letters and words. You might call them the vital components of reading. But this does not mean that they should be learned first, in isolation. Experience shows that learning letters and words can take place while the child is working with whole messages.

## Reading and writing
Hand in hand with this approach to reading goes early writing. Learning to express ideas in print certainly draws the child's attention to letters and words.

This dual approach—reading sentences on the one hand and learning to write messages on the other—does not ignore any of the time-honored methods of learning to read. Through it, a child can relate reading to talking: an important connection.

In addition it provides instant success for the learner. And in this field, as in others, nothing succeeds like success. The child who feels that he or she has made a good start *has* made a good start.

## What can I do?
There are many things you can do, in a practical way, to help your child to become a 'real' reader.

The suggestions we make in the next few chapters are based on our knowledge and observation of children who have become fluent and enthusiastic readers, and the information we have which is available from research. We believe that all parents have their children's future largely in their hands. So much development has already taken place before children enter school that the teacher's role can be viewed as only supplementary to what has gone before at home.

# 2  At home

Ideas about reading are more readily caught than taught in the very early years.

A youngster who grows up in a family where people read will come to feel that books and papers are worth attention. They certainly take attention away from him! Perhaps he will try to 'get into the scene' by crawling into Mom's lap, putting himself between the paper and his mother.

In the last fifty years or so, a great deal of thought and research has gone into the problem of why some children seem to learn quickly and easily at school, and others make little progress.

## Parents do matter

Throughout the world, researchers involved in the study of how children learn to read and write have been turning their attention from school to the home. An enormous amount of scholarly research supports the view that a child's early encounters with print at home have a tremendous effect on his or her later development at school. As Jerome Harste, Carolyn Burke and Virginia Woodward at Indiana University wrote in a 1982 report to the National Institute of Education:

Whether by design or default, children who were reported as always being 'drug around' on shopping trips, trips to the courthouse, trips to the doctor's office, trips anywhere, whether or not the trip seemingly matched the child's developmental interest, seemed to have an advantage. These same children who were reported as always 'under foot,' who naturally got included in cooking and setting the table, who were reported as writing out shopping lists and reading them during shopping, who were given paper and pen to write a letter to grandmother while the adult wrote letters or sent bills, who were given the occupant mail to open and read while the mother opened and read the rest of the mail, were seemingly at an advantage. Most of these activities had no great literacy teaching design behind them in the parent's eyes, but were done more by virtue of the fact that the child was about and involvement seemed natural largely because it was the only logical way the parent had for getting about the business of the day.

So you can see that when young children are exposed to print in the natural course of every-day life, they are developing a solid basis that will give them a great advantage when they start school.

A fascinating project was carried out by Dr. Margaret Clark in Glasgow (see *Young Fluent Readers*) in 1976. It has special interest for our purposes because it concentrates on the lives of thirty-two children all of whom could read by the time they entered school at five. These children came from different backgrounds; from the very wealthy, to the very poor. But they all came from families where books were read and stories were told. One little boy, whose father was an unskilled laborer, was the youngest of a family of seven. His older brothers and sisters had all learned to read easily, too. Questioning revealed that the father of the family, although he had left school at fourteen, loved fairy stories and had always told them to his children. Both he and his wife enjoyed reading, and had taken the children regularly to the public library. Although money was short the family owned books. No one had tried to teach the youngest child to read at this early age; surrounded by books and people who read for pleasure, he had learned.

All of these investigations were undertaken with the intention of discovering those factors which contribute to children's progress in learning to read. The evidence showed overwhelmingly that parents matter.

What does all this mean, in positive terms?

It means that from the earliest days parents, in our kind of society, should introduce their children to the world of books. They should read to them often and they should look closely at themselves as readers. They present a vital example for their children to copy.

Dr. Elizabeth Sulzby at Northwestern University wrote in a report to the National Council of Teachers of English:

In early reading development the parent structures storybook reading so that the child knows what it *feels like* to read a book with comprehension long before the child can perform the task alone. Unfortunately, not all children receive such early support in reading and, for some, early school experience does not build upon or provide such experiences.

## Parents as readers

Does your child see you reading books, as well as newspapers and magazines? Children in many modern homes may never see an adult concentrating for any considerable period of time on anything except the television screen! Pages of print can look forbidding to a child who cannot read. On the other hand, if a child sees a parent utterly absorbed by a book he or she is likely to feel that such an experience is worth striving towards. (A five-year-old girl we know snatched such a book from her father and, her eyes fixed with frutration on the incomprehensible text, said with some passion: 'Tell me what's in it! Read it to me!' She was certain that it must be fascinating. Dad hadn't taken his eyes off it for the last hour!)

Watching parents and others use books as part of their everyday activities helps a child to become a reader. Sharing in family letter writing and receiving can focus a child's attention on print, and its capacity to capture human speech. The idea that messages can come from marks on the page that other people have made with pen or pencil, encourages children to try their skill, at both 'getting' and 'sending' messages. This is one of the ways in which they start to learn about letters and words, as they need them, for their own purposes.

And it is not only in the field of reading and writing that the child will be forging ahead, in such a family. From earliest days, thoughtful parents can involve their child in learning that just seems to happen; learning that is fun.

## Finding opportunities

Try counting the learning points in the following exchanges, remembering that the mother might easily have said, sharply, 'Run away now, I want to read my letter'.

'Look Sally, a letter from Grandpa! Let's see what he says.'

(Almost certainly, Grandpa has written on the bottom 'Love to Sally' and this can be pointed out, examined and enjoyed.) Or:

'Here's a note to tell us to pay for the telephone. We'll go into the telephone company and pay it while we're shopping. See? It says we must pay...' (Or perhaps it's 'write a check and mail it'.)

Let's consider Grandpa's letter first:

★   People can 'talk' in one place and by writing their 'talking' onto paper make sure that another person 'hears' later.

★   People who are fond of one another keep in touch by doing this. Both enjoy it.

★   It is usual to answer a letter. Sometimes, a particular question needs an answer. Sometimes, one just chats.

Then the phone bill...

★ Again, it is possible to give people information by writing it down and mailing it.

★ The 'phone people' have to be paid, and there are several ways of doing this.

★ Identification of the Post Office and how it helps with sending messages. (Some preschoolers trail behind parents who never put them in the picture about *where* they are going, or *why*, or *where* they are when they get there.)

From such experiences, there will be a constant flow of information about envelopes, stamps, air letters, postcards, not to mention the growth of confidence which comes from knowing, progressively, how things work. You may be able to think of more learning points. The real point is that all this learning can proceed easily, gradually and inevitably if parents will only get into the habit of involving their children in the ordinary things of life.

And, for the particular purpose of this book the child's attention will be constantly directed at letters and words in their right and proper place, as part of messages, conveyed from one human mind to another.

All too often, parents think that preschool learning will require expensive equipment, or expenditure of time which they just don't have. Not so at all; the opportunities are there in any family situation, on the dullest day, with no special equipment. You must have noticed how preschoolers can't keep their hands off papers, objects, books and pens that are lying around! All too often this tremendous urge to inspect, to handle, to manipulate is attributed to sheer naughtiness.

Of course it's not! And if adults will only take the trouble to 'help' with this endless investigation into the fascinating ways of the world, the learning that takes place will be considerable. The youngster will learn to look closely, to handle carefully, to listen intently.

Back to family letters. Children love to receive letters of their own, long before they can read or write, and this is one way in which grandparents and others can help. 'Answering' the letter is fun and sometimes produces an astonishing result:

Stephanie aged four and her older sister and brother had received books from a relative as presents. The older children were writing thank you notes, and suggested that Stephanie draw a picture for inclusion in the envelope. Stephanie clearly felt unattracted to this idea. She found a sheet of lined paper. 'Write "Dear Aunty Jean",' she instructed her mother. This being done, she filled the page with 'writing', line after line, always starting at the left margin, keeping to the lines and using a neat, regular 'script' which bore an astonishing resemblance to 'real writing'.

Near the bottom, she stopped. 'Write "Love from Stephanie" now, please,' she requested.

Think how much this little girl knew already about letter writing:

★ Letters begin at the top with 'Dear So and So' (the person you wish to communicate with).

★ Letters end at the bottom with 'Love from' (whoever is writing).

★ Written language proceeds from left to right across the page, and from top to bottom of the page.

★ Lines on notepaper are there to help you keep your writing neat and orderly.

There was no doubt in Stephanie's mind that Aunt Jean would be pleased to read her letter, and none in ours that Stephanie was well on the way to mastering the intricacies of transforming speech into written symbols and re-converting it. That is, she was learning to read.

## Letters

From an early age children love knowing and identifying their own first initial and will practice writing it, often in strange or inappropriate places: Diana's mother was somewhat annoyed one day to find a bold if wobbly 'D' on the back of the sofa. The ensuing conversation is worth recording, for reasons other than those which this book is intended to serve.

**Mother** (irately): Who wrote 'D' on the back of the sofa?
**Diana**: In green crayon?
**Mother** (surprised): Yes...
**Diana** (firmly): Not me!

Once they recognize their own first initial of course, children seem to find it everywhere.

Stephen, aged four, came home from kindergarten with a large 'S' which he had written himself, on his painting. His three-year-old brother, Timothy wanted to know his 'letter' and was quite fascinated with the large 'T' his mother inscribed for him. Later he was seen to be crouched on the floor in the kitchen, his face against the boards, peering at a tiny engraved plate at the base of the refrigerator. Suddenly, in a muffled but triumphant voice he said, 'It's got one Stephen but it's got two Timmies!'

Alphabet charts which may be mounted or pinned up on the wall (low enough for the children to see them) are both attractive and useful for letter recognition. There are several clear and colorful versions on the market. Curiosity and learning can be stimulated by these, but a word of caution is not out of place.

Alphabets are sometimes used for rather dull routines. Saying the whole alphabet from A to Z is an achievement, but it has very little to do with reading and can lead the child to misunderstand what reading is. For example, one little girl could sing, and say the whole alphabet, but could recognize only five letters. When asked to learn a new letter her first response was 'a b c d ...' trailing off as she realized this did not help. Another child could name a letter in isolation, but only after he had very quickly whispered the whole alphabet up to that letter. An over-emphasis on letter names can make the learning of letter sounds difficult, and vice versa.

Avoid giving the child a rigid version of the role of each letter. Flexibility is what will help most of all.

Children can make lots of discoveries with a package of plastic letters which have little magnets set into them. Using a steel oven tray they can sort and arrange the ones they like best. Slowly, bit by bit, they will add to the groups of letters they know. A few favorite words can be learned in this way. Magnetic letters can be used in many different ways. Unlike an alphabet chart, they can be put down and taken apart. These activities appeal to young children.

Some children seem to love symbols, and once started, find them everywhere. 'Look Mommy, it's a big "O"' was one child's view of a circular table mat. Parents can help here, making the learning fun. A telephone pole looks like a 'T', a snake curls around like an 'S'. Children love to write large letters on wet sand at the beach. Their own natural curiosity, combined with their healthy instinct to experiment, probably provides the best key of all to good experiences with letters.

The same principle applies to figures. Young children can learn their 'own' number (age) and for fun, find it on the calendar and other places, and look forward to 'changing from 3 to 4' when their birthday comes. None of this instruction needs to take place in a 'teacher-pupil' way. In fact, this would probably spoil it. This sort of learning should happen incidentally, while everyday family life is going along.

Symbols are everywhere. Think of supermarkets, buses, street signs! The opportunity for a little 'fringe' learning is almost *always* present.

So far, this book seems to have fallen naturally into a question-and-answer pattern. It seems sensible to continue with this, if only for the reason that most of the questions individual parents ask are those which crop up time and again; questions to which complete answers can never be given because every child is different and every parent has his or her own way of looking at things. But most of them are the fundamental questions about young children and reading, and ought to be aired (if not answered), discussed, disputed if you like, but not dismissed. So let's continue.

We have already suggested that certain kinds of backgrounds are better for language learning, and for later reading, than others. If a child is to learn to read, it matters far less that a home should have carpet on the floor and two cars in the garage than that there should be people there who love him.

The connection is not immediately clear, but is there nonetheless. It is only too well recognized by teachers and social workers.

## Security and confidence

When young children move into the unfamiliar world of school, new behavior is expected of them. They need to be sure of themselves as people who matter if they are to be able to handle the challenges they will meet. When the going gets tough and self-doubt creeps in, they need their families to give them love and good humor, to relieve their tension; they need to feel that their family has confidence in them if they are to try again. Children need to *believe* that success is not beyond them.

Most children learn to read even though teachers use very different methods. But very few children learn to read without some struggle. Now and then the task is hard. Then it is the confident child who keeps trying, because she knows she has won through in the past. If a child has been made to feel a failure he or she will expect to fail when something looks strange and new. The child who has been allowed to try things for him or herself, has been encouraged with patience and praise, will carry those experiences to school. They will support him time and time again in the tasks that lie ahead.

If this sounds odd, you should think about the six-year-old facing a new teacher who asks him to read a book he has never seen before. He stumbles through the first line or two. The teacher prompts him. Now he is confused and he is beginning to panic. If he has had success in the past he may steady himself, feeling that he can do it. He may say to the teacher, 'I'll start again,' adding, 'all by myself,' to prevent the teacher interrupting. He takes responsibility for the task and can cope with the stress.

Boys or girls who have little confidence may have been criticized and made to feel failures. They will probably behave quite differently in this situation. They may shut out the teacher's voice *and help*, and deprive themselves of the chance to learn something new.

There is an important lesson here for the parents of preschool children. Be sure to arrange challenges for your children which they can meet; they need the experience of success. Make certain that tasks are geared to their present level. Choose a simpler jigsaw puzzle, for example, if they clearly can't manage a ten or twelve-piece. Do this subtly, watching for signs of frustration or loss of confidence. Later, they'll 'try and try again' if their early experiences have been rewarding ones.

If, on the other hand, they have been 'allowed' to fail continually on small undertakings, and particularly if they sense your anxiety or disappointment over their level of achievement, they may well refuse to try for fear of failing again. All too often, such children later feel threatened by the possibility of failing with reading. Sensing adult opinion that reading is *very* important, they may pretend boredom, make fun of the task as too young for them, re-cast themselves as 'physical' types who want only to climb trees or throw balls. In short, they adopt a face-saving line of action which separates them from books.

Parents need sensitivity here. A child who is anxious about reading is a child at risk, and needs a crash course in acceptance and love. Comparison of different children's attainments, too many anxious inquiries about a particular child's progress, ill-judged home teaching (often using up precious time which might be devoted to story reading, or interesting conversation) can all impede, rather than accelerate progress.

This is not to underestimate the help that supportive parents can give a child who is found to be having real difficulties. A parent who is in tune with his or her child's way of learning, who is prepared to be patient and interested without being anxious or judging, can be the very person to give the individual time and attention that a child needs.

And remember, young children *want* to be like their parents. If you read, your preschoolers will want to copy you. But they need to be 'plugged in and switched on' early in life if the habit is to endure. Tragically, people who learn to read later in life seldom become mature readers, with all the commitment and satisfaciton which this term implies. True, their lives may be transformed by the ability to read simple prose, instructions, directories, street names and the like. It must never be thought to be too late to learn to read. But think what pleasures such a person has missed. We want more than this for our up-and-coming generation of preschoolers.

# Health and reading

This is perhaps a good chance to insert a reminder about physical factors, and the way in which they can help or retard a child's learning.

From earliest days, parents should observe their babies and children closely. Is their eyesight good? Do they hear normally with both ears? Ear trouble interferes with language learning. Even in families where the standard of child care is high, parents may be astonished to discover, only when a child is having difficulty with reading, that there is a problem with one or other of these senses.

Poor diet is not always associated with low income; often parents need to look closely at family eating habits if their children are not to suffer. Poor eating often leads to fatigue and the lowering of resistance to infection. And lowered intelligence can accompany malnutrition.

In families where all these factors are considered, some children will, nonetheless, be more frail, and have more frequent illnesses than others. These children need special thought, as well as special attention and treatment. If a child is physically weaker than the average child or physically handicapped, help to compensate by developing habits and hobbies which may allow the child to forge ahead intellectually, to understand the world even if he or she cannot move around it easily. All too often 'missing school' is given later as an excuse for poor reading and low achievement. Make the extra time spent at home an opportunity for *more* conversation, *more* stories read aloud, *more* games played. Make sure that other family members understand the child's need for involvement with people and for one-to-one help in mastering skills.

Astonishing results have been achieved by families who would not accept the gloomy predictions of professionals!

Mental handicaps are harder than any other sort of handicap to assess in infancy, and perhaps hardest of all for parents to accept. Mentally handicapped childrens' needs are exactly those of all children, but they may be harder to meet. They need love, acceptance, humor and the opportunity to learn. Your satisfaction in the child will be in proportion to your investment in his care. We have seen parents of an eighteen-months-old child who has just learned to clap her hands after weeks of teaching, quite carried away with joy. Their 'normal' baby learned this skill, almost unnoticed, and certainly untaught, at eight months. But the *real* joy was attached to the older child's achievement.

Don't assume that the child will never read. Make books a part of life from earliest babyhood. The book can be one of your tools in forging a relationship with the child. Whatever level he or she can possibly reach will become more accessible with your care. Let books be a joyful help to you both!

# 3  Books, books, books

There is clear evidence that it matters more what a child brings to the task of learning to read than what the teacher has to offer him. In fact, if a child comes to the task not sufficiently equipped, the teacher is obliged to try to make up for this lack of resources before real reading instruction can begin.

It amounts to this (and we are putting this in capital letters, in the hope that parents will commit it to memory and make it an important operating principle); IN READING, WHAT THE BRAIN SAYS TO THE EYE MATTERS MORE THAN WHAT THE EYE SAYS TO THE BRAIN.

Frank Smith is the author of that principle, and of some interesting books on reading. The principle is that a child needs a mind that is well-stocked; a mind that is active. And it means that parents have a responsibility to help their children develop this sort of mind.

This is where children's story books come in. There is no substitute for reading and telling stories to children, from the very earliest days.

## Cushla and Carol

It seems that a child is almost never too young to be introduced to books. Cushla, a multi-handicapped, chronically-ill baby who needed constant care was shown pictures in books and read to from four months of age. Her progress through a babyhood and early childhood over-shadowed with illness, and dotted with crises, confounded doctors who had predicted a future of severe retardation for her. Today, at six and a half Cushla is reading at a level well beyond her actual age. She still has all her original handicaps. The doctors were certainly not wrong about these! Their predictions fell down because they had no way of knowing that Cushla's family would make sure that her contact with language and books become a central part of her life. No one has had to 'teach' Cushla the mechanics of reading. In a climate of language and stories, Cushla *learned!*

A healthy child's interaction with books is recorded in a fascinating diary kept by a mother from the time her daughter was two years old, until school entry at five. *Books Before Five* by Dorothy Neal White is an important book. (Unfortunately, it is now out of print but you might find it in a library.) Through its pages, one follows Carol's almost daily contact with new ideas, fresh situations, previously unknown words and concepts. When Carol was just over two, her mother wrote:

The experience makes the book richer, and the book enriches the personal experience even at this level. I am astonished at the early age this backward and forward flow between books and life takes place. With adults or older children, one cannot observe it so easily, but here at this age when all a child's experiences are known and the books read are shared, when the voluble gabble which in her speech reveals all the associations, the interaction is seen very clearly.

## How to get books

First books are of course picture books, and we anticipate an immediate question. Parents of preschoolers may be at a stage where the available money will not stretch to all the necessities, let alone luxuries. Perhaps you are on the way to seeing books as high on the necessity list, but this may take time. Let's face the obvious question: How can parents afford to provide their children with enough books at the preschool level?

Libraries cater more and more to the needs of the very young child. (This, in itself, is proof that it is now recognized that books matter to children.) However, many parents are reluctant to borrow from libraries because they fear that their toddlers may damage books. This is such a near-certainty that librarians just have to accept it, and do, increasingly. Parental care can usually help, but the honest wear and tear occasioned by clumsy over-eager little hands is expected and accepted, in most children's departments of public libraries.

Some of the most personal, and therefore most beloved, books in a preschooler's life can, of course, be home-made. Collect colorful, clear pictures of familiar objects from magazines and other sources, and make a scrapbook. If you wish, stick the pictures on firm cardboard, cover each page with clear plastic, and tie the 'pages' of the book together loosely, with colored string or yarn. A scrapbook serves very well as a 'show and tell' sort of book, and it has the advantage of being a very personal possession.. The fact that pictures may be added from time to time gives it a unique quality. And even very small toddlers will sense that you are making something special for them.

And don't forget about 'made up' stories, told spontaneously as the need arises. Often, these stories become family favorites, requested again and again. Naturally, the characters include the child who is listening, wide-eyed and delighted when 'who should come round the corner with his friend the dragon, but David!'

There is significance in the fact that many people have submitted such stories to publishers and been disappointed when they proved 'not of suitable standard'. 'But my child *loved* the stories about Leander the Goat, or Penelope the Hen', the puzzled would-be author protests. Of course the child did, and rightly so! What could be more heart-warming and stirring than your very *own* story, from your very *own* father, with *yourself* appearing in the nick of time to save the day? (This is not, of course, to discount the likelihood of any of these stories achieving publication. Think of 'Pooh Bear' and 'Alice'.) Your creation need not be of high literary merit to impress and delight your child.

The conversation which arises from this one-to-one story session is a priceless asset. Any way of increasing child-adult language contact should be valued. It is here that a child learns the way in which language *works*, the ways in which ideas may be considered, modified, expanded...

Always encourage your child to express his ideas, and try to listen respectfully, however falteringly he speaks. You can help with interested questions which

will depend on what you know of him, and his capacity. 'That must have been exciting! What happened next?' may be all that is necessary to keep a rather bumbling recounter of an incident at kindergarten going. The keynote is 'interest', against a background of *time* and *attention*, allowing him to experiment with ways of saying what he means.

## Paperbacks will help

The modern paperback publishing industry has transformed book-ownership for millions of people throughout the world, not the least of them children. A very large range of excellent, beautifully illustrated books is now available and these are, in contrast to hard-covered picture books, on sale in many local stores and shops.

The very reasonable price of these books brings them within the range of all families who are determined to provide books for their children. Careful covering (with clear plastic, to preserve the cover illustration and title), and judicious reinforcing and repair with Scotch tape inside, can prolong the life and attractiveness of picture paperbacks and ensure that the initial cost is well justified.

But owning a beautiful hard-covered book is important, too. A good collection of Nursery Rhymes, an anthology of simple stories, an alphabet book and a counting book; these are bread-and-butter items which the preschool child should have on hand always. New books, some of which he may have met for the first time through the library, will be worth the allocation of family funds, from time to time. A mother reports:

Victoria and Andrew (4 and 3) loved *Mike Mulligan and his Steam Shovel* on first reading from the library. We renewed it and renewed it. In vain did I explain that other children might like to borrow it. In the end, I managed to buy a copy. I was almost tempted to give the *new* copy to the library. We had really left our mark on the old!

Vicky and Andrew are grown up, but a battered copy of *Mike* still graces the family shelves. And several phrases from that well-loved story still occur in the family's private language.

A beloved, well-produced book will be treasured and kept. Strangely enough, for all their apparent flimsiness, children's hardback books do tend to survive. In many homes they are there still, years after the dolls' carriages, bikes and scooters of childhood have all disappeared.

## Listening to stories

You may agree that books are 'good for preschoolers', but wonder about how this works towards reading. For example: How exactly does listening to stories help children when they later start to learn to read?

It is certain that listening to stories expands the vocabulary. The speech of children who are used to 'book language' is often rich and varied. This is easy to understand; such children have a large stock of words and ideas to draw on.

This stock just has to help when they are later trying to make sense of a line of print. They need resources to call on, then. How can a beginning reader, groping for a word, find it unless it is in his or her mind to begin with?

Helen had been at school for a week, and was glorying in her apparent ability to 'read'. Lying on the floor at home, with admiring family around her, she flipped over the pages of her 'pre-reader'.
'This is a red ball,' she said with confidence.
'This is a red door.'
'This is a red coat...'
The next page showed a red van, and this stopped her in her tracks.
It wasn't a *car* and it wasn't a *truck*...Her gaze swung backwards and forwards between the picture and the text. It settled on the text and she was seen to be conjuring up all her resources...An older sister was called Victoria, so she knew 'V'...'This is a red "VEHICLE"!' came out in a triumphant shout.

Wrong...? Let's just report that this was a child who learned to read very quickly — a child whose mind *was* well-equipped with words and ideas. Remember, what the brain says to the eye is very important.

A young reader was being introduced to a book called *The Thin King and the Broth*. He said, 'What's broth?' The teacher didn't tell him, but she invited him to think by saying, 'You remember "There was an old woman who lived in a shoe, she had..." 'I know,' he said, 'I know,' and he was still thinking, struggling to grasp the idea he had just discovered and to put it into words. 'Soup!' he cried, as if he had made the exciting discovery of a new word all by himself.

The new word was 'broth', and he had been helped to link it to a meaning he already knew very well. Searching the mind for meanings has a great deal to do with reading.

That is the essence of sensitive teaching. Not to tell, not to drill, not merely to reward with approval, but to bring children to the point where, on their own, they can search and check, and work out messages for themselves.

There is another major way in which the child who is used to hearing stories read aloud is being helped towards reading. Has it ever occurred to you that 'book language' is quite different from the spoken language of everyday conversation? Not the actual words, but their arrangement in sentences and paragraphs. When we are chatting to one another, we constantly break off, gesture with our hands, alter or enlarge our meaning by the use of facial expressions, change the direction our sentence was taking, all without losing our listener's understanding. This is because the person we are talking to is picking up cues from our total behavior, not merely from our speech.

Books, on the other hand, have to rely upon words and sentences alone, and so the language is arranged in a particular way — a way with which the child needs to be familiar. He is used to it if he has been read to, constantly, since babyhood. In fact, this accounts for the fact that many 'well-read-to' preschoolers speak in more complex sentences than children who have had to rely on spoken language alone for their example.

And when reading begins at school...well, imagine a child who has never heard fairy stories read aloud trying to decipher 'Once upon a time'!

Having some of the patterns of book language in the mind to fit language into, is just as important as knowing what the words mean.

## Other experiences

Children need opportunities to arrange their own lives, to organize their own experiences, to put their own behavior together and establish order in their own world. And this implies the freedom to do this. What has this to do with reading? In the end no one can help the reader. Children must explore the text, respond to it, re-create the story, find their own mistakes, correct them, and read on. They must organize their own behavior.

Many of their past experiences in play will have prepared them for this control over what they are trying to do.

Play is recognized by leading authorities in the educational field as having tremendous value for children. In their play, be it with pots and pans from the kitchen cupboard, sand, water, earth, blocks, cars, dolls and all the paraphernalia of housekeeping, they are constantly extending their knowledge of the world and how it works. Cause and effect, comparison, trial and error, the give-and-take of relationships with other people, all are experienced and re-experienced. Children learn in play how to manipulate their environment and test their growing skills, physical, intellectual and social, against the many demands of their environment.

Books about play can help here. You will find several titles described in the last chapter of this book.

## Will all this really help?

We believe that it will. We need to repeat here that reading is *not* merely de-coding symbols into words

and repeating them one after the other. *Meaning* has to emerge, before a child is truly reading. Reading is re-creating, almost without knowing one is doing it, from known words and concepts, drawing conclusions from what has gone before, looking forward with imagination to what may be expected to follow. The process is helped enormously if the child has had the opportunity to be creative in the past.

This might be a good place to insert a thought which seems to us to have a lot to say about making sure that all children move naturally into the reading process. It is this:

To live a rich, full and satisfying life at each stage of growth is the best possible preparation for the next stage.

# 4  More direct instruction

The suggestions that follow should not be used as a starting point. The foundation-building outlined in earlier chapters is essential if these ideas are to work.

Also, the steps we describe here will not conflict with instruction which the child will later encounter. There are certain things which the beginning reader has to absorb and master before progress can be made, regardless of the instruction system used. Knowing these things is certain to help.

Well, there you are with a four-year-old, who has been read to, talked to and listened to since very early days. She is speaking well, has a considerable attention span, enjoys a wide range of play experiences, and you want to take her a step further along the road to 'real reading'.

## How do I start?

It's a good idea to observe carefully what the child *does* know about books. Adults take for granted many things that children have to learn. Use this as a checklist:

★ Do they know that a book starts at the front and proceeds, page by page, to the back? (Have them show you the 'front' and the 'back'.)

★ Do they know that the spoken words, as the story is read to them, arise from the black marks, the print, on the page?

★ Do they know that the print must be 'read' from left to right across the page?

★ Do they know that, if there is more than *one* line of print, we read the top one first, then the next down, and so on?

It helps if the child has heard terms like 'word', 'letter', 'print' and 'title' used casually during story sessions, and at other times. This happens so naturally in a 'reading' family that teaching such concepts in unnecessary. But check, nonetheless. It is surprising how easily children who are read to seem to slip into this knowledge, but there may be some confusion, which can be resolved. You may find that the child does not want to cooperate, despite a healthy 'reading' background. No matter. Many children with a fund of this sort of knowledge, children who have not received any 'instruction' before school, get off to a fine start when school begins.

On Joanna's first day at school, the children were asked to draw a picture showing something that they had done during the vacation.

The teacher then wrote a sentence, dictated by the children, under each picture.

On arrival home Joanna proudly showed her mother a picture under which the teacher had written 'I went on an escalator in a big store'. 'That word says "escalator",' Joanna told her mother confidently, pointing correctly.

'How do you know?' asked her mother. 'Because "escalator" is a big word, and that word is the biggest,' said Joanna.

This five-year-old had had no preschool instruction in reading, but had been read to constantly. Obviously, 'a word' was a recognizable unit of print on the page to Joanna. It was possible to make inferences from existing knowledge, and she did so.

Back to the four-year-old whom we introduced at the beginning of this section. You have checked her understanding of the 'book facts' we have just listed, you have found her in satisfactory shape, and decide to proceed. We suggest the following steps for the parent:

★ Choose a familiar book with a brief and very easy text, clearly displayed on the page. As an alternative, or as well, you might like to make your own book, perhaps using the child's ideas for the text. But *keep it very very simple*; preferably, one short sentence occupying one line only on each page, with related picture. (Many parents choose material that is far too difficult.)

★ Read several pages slowly to the child, running your finger under the words as you say them.

★ Increase the number of pages treated in this way as you judge her interest to be increasing.

★ Read several different and very easy books (printed or homemade) in this way, repeating the performance and re-using the same books as often as the child seems interested.

If all is going well you should now be able to progress to the following:

★ Using one of the now familiar children's books, choose a short sentence and have the child repeat this after you, while you underline the words with your finger. (If possible, for this first attempt, find a page with one simple sentence only on it.) Initially, do this for only one or two pages. Gradually increase the number of pages for which the child joins in, but only if her interest in helping increases.

★ Read several books in this way, and re-read the old ones.

★ The next step may be taken spontaneously by the child, or you may suggest it; that is, that she might underline the words with *her* finger while saying them, after you.

Remember, however, that the young child may not have sufficient control of her small muscles to do this, or may tire easily. No matter. Knowing that this has something to do with stories and reading is enough.

And please! If you feel yourself getting discouraged, angry or impatient, negative in any way, do give up and return to story sessions only. Remember that reading is an extremely complicated act, and that you probably think it a great deal simpler for your child than it is. At all costs you must avoid associating learning to read with unpleasantness, strain, or boredom.

It is probably a sound idea to finish each 'teaching' session with a *real* story (*not* a graded reader) of the child's choice. If you are handling things well, she may delight herself (and you) by ultimately finding a familiar word or expression quite spontaneously in one of her picture books. This is fine, if it happens, but pressing for it may spoil the relaxed pleasures she has always had from stories, and do more harm than good.

This stage can be maintained for a considerable period of time. In fact the benefits will increase with repetition. The child will be constantly *drawing her own conclusions* about letters, words and sentences, and the way they all fit together to tell stories.

The following anecdote was supplied by a parent who suddenly realized that her child had been doing exactly this. She had certainly had no intention of 'teaching' him.

Kevin loved *Davy's Day* from babyhood, and would often ask for it even after he had turned three — particularly when he was tired. Each page has a simple statement about Davy's everyday doings, near the top of the page. (The text is consistently on the left page, with picture on the right.) On most pages there is one word at the bottom of the page, well away from the rest of the text, which gives a lead into the sentence on the next page. On four of the pages this word is 'and', on another four 'or', and on two pages 'then'. On one single page, right at the end of the book, the two words 'and soon' occur in this position. I had always pointed to these words with a flourish, stressing them for expression really. To my astonishment, when he was about three I discovered one day that Kevin knew these words. Several times, he found them in other books we were reading together.

This mother continued:

I thought of trying to teach him more words, but couldn't be bothered! He seemed to be learning words and expressions constantly from our read-aloud sessions — I think I have always been inclined to point to the print as I read.

There was certainly no real intention to 'teach' in this mother's behavior, for she concludes:

I love books myself and have always read a lot to the children. It's so much more peaceful than what goes on if I let them get bored and ill-tempered!

## Where do I go from here?

Some parents may still feel that they want to involve their children in a more definite teaching program, and might like to introduce the 'sentence game' at this stage. Here's how to go about it.

★  Make a very small number of 'word cards', using ordinary cardboard. The back of a used writing pad will do well; cut long strips about 1 inch deep and snip off the length you need for each word.

★  Use simple words which will have meaning and interest for your child. For example, if you have a boy and a girl, you might try these words: Paul / Susan / is / a / boy / girl.

★  Next, arrange the cards to make a sentence, encouraging the child to help. The first sentence should feature his own name: 'Paul is a boy'.

The second will, of course, be 'Susan is a girl'. Without any more cards, you can have some fun. Let him correct you when you write 'Paul is a girl' or 'Susan is a boy'. In a very short time, he will differentiate between 'boy' and 'girl' and be able to select the other words as needed.

He may like to keep the words in a box, using them whenever he wishes. When you use the words, use them only in sentences, to preserve the 'message' value of print.

Now continue, using you own family situation and consolidating *always* before adding more words. If your family (or a relative's or neighbor's family) includes a baby — or a cat, dog, or other pet — you have plenty of opportunity to extend the game without changing its form:

'Martin is a baby.'
'Patch is a dog.'

★  This might be a good time to point out that he really needs more 'is' and 'a' cards — a painless way of helping him to realize that these small words occur very often in English. The word 'and', of course, is the obvious next choice, so that he can join two or more sentences together.

★  Once he is really used to making these sentences, another 'form' can be introduced. Once again, it can be fun:

'Paul likes cake.'
'Martin likes milk.'
'Patch likes bones.'

The words in these new sentences can then be interchanged, while the word 'likes' and the names of various foods are learned.

Inevitably, the child will ask you to make more cards — and some of them will not be very simple

words at all! Some children want to start making their own cards quite soon. A four-year-old we know was so insistent upon this that her mother started cutting up cereal boxes into very large cards so that her daughter could print on them with her crayons. Later, this child even cut her own cards. Their uneven shapes, with her very wobbly printing, proved no hindrance to learning. In the end, they were all housed in a large cardboard carton.

You will have the idea by now, and will be able to introduce new forms gradually. You might try 'is' (card already familiar) followed by an adjective: 'Paul is big', 'Martin is little', 'Patch is black'.

You can see that the next words might be 'not' and 'very'! But, stay with simple and easy texts, don't let it become complicated! Enterprising preschoolers can play the game together, or with an adult. Before long, quite lengthy sentences emerge.

We would expect our four-year-old to forget as easily as he or she learns and not always to know tomorrow what he or she knew yesterday. This should not worry you, or the child.

Do not expect that this skill in sentence making and word selecting, or an interest in letters, will immediately carry over into reading books. Children differ greatly here, and many who seem slow to make the transfer become excellent readers in the end. The value of this contact with the way written language works to convey meaning to the reader will not be lost; it is fundamental to the reading process. Many children who have been tutored on individual words in isolation have missed this foundation. Often their parents are puzzled by their failure to make progress, but it is not surprising.

An interesting illustration of how one kind of learning can block another kind of learning from happening came to our notice recently. The mother of a preschooler taught her little boy to recognize 300 words before he went to school. That was an unusually large list and they must have worked as a wonderful teaching-learning team. After he had been at school for a year the mother went to discuss his lack of progress with the teacher. The mother could not understand why he was not moving more rapidly through the school program. The teacher asked the boy to read one of the earliest and simplest reading books. On continuous text in the story book, he could not read. He had the wrong idea about reading. He thought he was supposed to find that word 'in his head' from his 300 words, and say it. He did not understand that all the skills he had for speaking could help him anticipate words following one another in the story. He did not know that the plot could also guide him, and that the letters could give him cues. For him reading was flash recognition of a snapshot view of a word. This can be a starting point for some children who then learn to use other ways of getting to accurate reading. But this little boy was so good at word recognition, and he had practiced it for so long, that his first reaction was to 'word call' and he found it very difficult to remember that reading involves many other things. Even when he remembered he found it difficult to be flexible, because well-established habits have a way of controlling us.

The rule is to introduce words *in sentences* always, encouraging the child to use a full range of cues and clues to get the meaning from print. This is what reading is all about.

A note of caution! Don't institute the sentence

game *instead* of the 'reading together' sessions described earlier in this chapter. Continue with both, simultaneously, if they are being enjoyed.

More importantly, don't use up precious time on either, at the expense of reading aloud from exciting picture books. Knowing beyond any doubt that reading is fun is the only certain inducement for the child to keep going!

# 5 Parents' questions

In this chapter we will try to answer some of the questions parents ask about modern teaching methods, and about their own role in their child's education.

Many of the answers (and questions) involve repetition of what has gone before, but we feel that this does not matter; if a point is worth making it is worth making *twice* (at least).

Parents are, understandably, puzzled about methods that they do not understand. Often they feel that there is no method being used.

Many parents have these doubts. Because they sat in desks at an earlier period and worked steadily through a reading course, they feel that this is the right way. 'We learned this way,' they say, 'What's wrong with it?'

Our answers in this section are based on the proposition that teaching methods should fit in with, and support, the learning process at every stage. We hope that no one will disagree with that!

## Is the teaching of reading today quite different from what it was, say, fifty years ago?

Not really. Dramatic claims are often made, and people may be persuaded to believe that children were once 'really taught' to read, in a serious way, whereas now teachers 'play around' with 'new methods'.

In the days when 'phonics' as a method was said to be used exclusively, this was not so. Anyone who is fifty will be able to remember labelled pictures on the wall, the new word each day used in a sentence, illustrated books with stories in them, and many other 'aids'. In the same way, during the Dick and Jane era of the 1950s when whole words were emphasized, teachers found that they naturally drew children's attention to letters and sounds. The children would otherwise have had a serious handicap in attacking new words.

What we hope is that teachers today are using sensibly the findings of modern research on reading. The best features of all the so-called 'methods' have value and a place in a well-balanced program. Labels like 'phonic' methods or 'look-and-say' methods are too simple. They distort the rich programs they are supposed to describe.

## How do children learn to identify new words?

Only a few new words are introduced at a time, and the teacher arranges a series of learning steps. To begin with, she will make sure that the children know what each word means. Then she will read a story containing the new words, so that the children hear them in the context of a message. That is their 'real' place.

When the child then reads the same material, he is prepared for the new words, and is able to succeed in recognizing them. When reading aloud material that contains a new word that he has not been prepared for, the child will be encouraged to anticipate what the new word might be. The structure of the sentence and the sense of the story often lead to a correct idea. If the child checks on the first letter of the word as well, he will usually be correct in his response. We do this all the time as adult readers. You can catch yourself at it, next time you are faced by a newspaper article in which a few words, or a whole line of print has been omitted.

But the teacher is not merely letting the child guess when she invites him to try a word he has not met before. She will not be content even if he is correct. She is then likely to say, 'Are you right? How did you know?' encouraging the child to look closely at the method he used to identify the word. Perhaps he knew the first letter, and guessed, perhaps also sensing that the word's 'sounded' length matched its written length. He may have done these things without knowing he did. This happens all the time in a complex mental operation like reading. Identifying the method he used may help him to use it again, extending and modifying it as required.

If you have not thought about this process before, you might like to have a little more detail about how it works. We might call it the 'new-word identification process' or 'reading through context'.

The first clues that a child picks up about a new word come from the sentence itself. 'The boy threw the...' 'The old man climbed...up the hill'. The missing word in the first sentence will be a noun. In the second sentence the word will probably be an adverb ending in 'ly'.

Even without the story to help us we might guess that the first sentence needs a word like 'ball', or 'stone', or something like 'boy', or 'thief' or, as a long shot, 'teacher'. It can only be one of a very few words. In the second sentence the most likely word is probably 'slowly', but you could think of others.

When you are reading a story a new word can only be one of a small number of words. (We forget this when we think that reading is being able to read words in isolation.)

Now, if the child reader notices that the first sentence has 'The boy threw the b...', she is using a 'first letter' clue. There may only be two or three likely words to fit everything she has noticed so far. At the same time she considers word length, without actually counting letters and discards 'bed' and 'balloon'. Her eye picks up the last letter 'l' and putting all together she says 'bell'. She might be wrong, because the boy may have been playing with a football, and our reader would then have a sentence that did not make sense with other parts of the story. If so she would probably take a closer look, say the word slowly letter by letter (or letter group by letter group) and discover for herself the point of her error.

This sounds complicated but it isn't. You may have noticed that it works a little like the game 'Twenty Questions', because each bit of information reduces the number of ideas to be considered. And the brain works very fast in sorting out the possibilities.

What could our reader have learned? This may well have been a critical experience for her. It may have taught her that first and last letters are not entirely

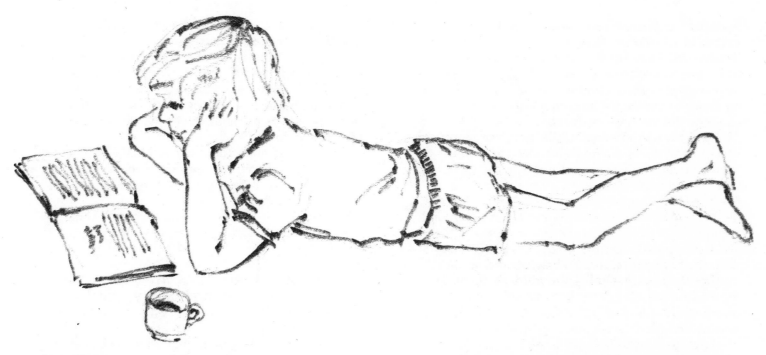

reliable, and that it is important to work slowly from left to right across a word to distinguish it from a very similar word (bell, ball).

What might you have learned from this example? That there are many, many occasions when you are reading text when it is not necessary to take in all the information. Like the 'Twenty Questions' game, you do not always need all the questions.

You may think 'What a complicated way to teach. Why not just teach the child to sound the letters, or recognize the words?' There is a vast amount of evidence to convince us that the brain works on reading in this way and that it does this whatever teaching program is used. It does not matter what method the teachers adopt: observers find children acting in this way, regardless.

This is the way adults read. It is a way by which very young children who don't know many words can read interesting but simple stories. A child can add to his own knowledge, if he approaches print in this way. And that is very important. He still has to know a great deal about letter-sound relationships, and he goes on learning this until he is ten or twelve years old. He learns eventually to recognize words in a flash, but that is because he has read them so many times. They are very familiar to him.

## What if my child seems slow to move on from this early stage?

Parents do not worry too much if their children are a little slow to walk or cut their teeth. They accept this as part of the range of individual differences among children. For the same kinds of reasons some children will be slower to reach the stage where they can begin to learn to read. Children differ quite markedly in the speed and ease with which they learn to read.

It helps the child who is moving slowly if we can feel comfortable about individual differences and neither worry about it ourselves nor worry the child about it. Don't make an issue of it. Encourage the child, give praise for what he can do, protect him from the jibes of brothers and sisters and unhappy comparisons that he himself might be inclined to make. Talk the situation over with the teacher and help him to make real progress, little by little, however gradual. Don't panic, push or show anxiety. Forcing the pace will not help and may do great damage. He can only proceed from where he is.

## Should I hear the child's reading at home?

Opinions differ about the usefulness of hearing reading at home and you should be guided by the school's views.

If you are expected to help, you should consult the teacher about what you and your child can do together.

At all costs, resolve to make it relaxed, even 'fun', not a 'duty' session. Be positive and helpful when the child is 'stuck'.

'Have you looked at this part?'
'Would you like me to tell you?'
'Let's go back here and try that again.'

If the going gets too difficult, offer to read a few pages for the child. She will read it better tomorrow if she has heard how it all goes together today. It is easy to sound as if you are trying to trip her up instead of help her!

Use your own judgement about whether you should abandon the session, particularly if you feel that, despite your best intentions, a note of strain is creeping into the encounter.

And follow the session by reading aloud from an enjoyable picture book or collection of stories.

## What should I do if, despite everything, I feel very concerned that my child is not making progress in the first year?

If you are really concerned, teachers may let you observe their teaching your child at school. You may well be able to help at home, but if your child finds reading difficult then it is very important not to confuse him or her with different methods.

Your problem is that you will have a host of personal beliefs about reading and you will set out to teach your child what you believe he or she should be learning. You have the tremendous advantage of a one-to-one teaching situation, and the massive disadvantage of being personally involved in an emotional way, which means you will get irritated rather quickly. You will find it difficult to notice when the child has solved the problem in a different or unexpected way or made a significant learning gain in an area you didn't arrange for.

An experienced teacher will work in a flexible way to allow children who are different to approach reading along different routes. This may confuse you as a parent. Your Johnny may be doing different things from your friend's Mary in the same classroom. Don't panic. He may be too experienced in Mary's area to make it worth his spending time on her activities.

## Shouldn't children read accurately, without any mistakes?

Well, yes if they are already readers, but no, if they are learning to read. Let's go back to the idea of a self-improving system, the idea that the more a child reads the better she becomes. How would the system improve itself if it didn't have some difficulties for the reader to learn from? No more than one word out of every twenty should provide difficulty: any more would be discouraging. After an error has been made, the child often recognizes this and tries to correct it. This has been called self-correction. It shows you clearly that the child is applying her 'Twenty Questions' technique. It is part of the self-improving system because that is the moment when the child attends closely and discovers new things about print that she was overlooking before. We do it when we're reading the paper, but we do it silently.

The real goal is, of course, not accurate saying of the words but accurate reception of the message being read. The print on the page must be related by the child to some meaning from her past experience. To get from print to meaning we want the child, even the beginning reader, to think about what she is

reading, to react to it, to get ideas from it, and to link these ideas with other ideas from her memory of other experiences.

### In the light of what has been said so far, should parents try to teach their preschoolers to read?

We believe that adults should proceed cautiously, using methods like those described in the last section. You may be surprised to hear that there are studies to show that slightly older brothers and sisters have more success teaching preschoolers to read than parents do. And this should make us ask why.

We suspect that, without giving it any thought, slightly older children assess the real nature of the task better than adults. They have more recently grappled with it themselves, perhaps. Adults, many years past this stage, are inclined to judge the wrong things to be simple. There is a message here. We adults may be wrong about what we think the child needs to know, to read.

### Will my child start to learn to read on his first day at school?

From the day when the teacher first accepts your child into his class, his efforts will be directed towards teaching the child to read.

This is a time for settling, on your child's part, and observing on the teacher's. He needs to know 'where she is' before he can purposely take her 'somewhere else'. It is not hard to imagine the diversity of levels that teachers find in new entrants. Modern teaching tries to treat each child as an individual with special needs.

Before long your child will probably work with the help of small paperbacks which have a picture on one page at each opening, and a few words (usually a simple phrase or sentence) on the opposite page.

These books are sometimes called 'instant readers' or 'pre-primers' because, with the help of the picture and the first sentence of the book, the child is able to invent sentences like those in the book.

A teacher responding to the strengths of each child, will introduce them to formal reading sessions at different times. But you can rest assured that reading as a goal for each child looms large in the teacher's mind!

### Is it true that most schools have a 'reading readiness' program?

Your child may know a great deal about books when he or she comes to school. But not all children are well prepared. So the teacher introduces activities which allow her to observe which children can handle a book, open it, turn the pages, find and keep the place by the pictures, look from left to right across a page. The children learn how to study the details of pictures. Some have not yet learned to do this. They need practice at expressing in words the ideas suggested by the pictures. Their attention is directed to things that look alike and things that look different in the pictures, because they are being led towards looking for such differences in letters. Habits of noticing small differences are very important in learning words, but they are easily learned if we begin with objects and pictures rather than letters.

One little line makes all the difference between 'cat' and 'eat'.

## How can children learn if they are not made to sit quietly and pay attention to what the teacher says?

The atmosphere in schools is more informal today than when some of us went to school, but there is order, control and discipline which you may have a chance to observe. Many of the activities that prepare a child for reading involve talking. The teacher provides situations in which children will want to talk because they have something interesting to talk about. It is not just the willing talkers that concern the teacher. He or she must see that every child feels comfortable with language in this classroom.

As children gain experience in expressing themselves they gain the kind of control over words that helps them to anticipate and understand the language of books. Talking things over informally before and after reading is important in helping children get the most out of what they read.

You can see that 'sitting quietly' may be the very thing that most young children do *not* need. They learn best through being involved. Modern teachers try to provide this involvement for all children.

## I believe that children draw pictures and try to write before they can even read. Is this helpful?

When the child shows his picture to the teacher she may ask him to tell her about it. Then she will write down his dictated message for him. The child has made the statement in pictures; he puts the same message into words and the teacher writes this down. This is to help the child understand that messages can be put into print, and that print therefore has messages in it.

But very soon the child begins to trace the teacher's message or to copy it. And when he is sufficiently confident he may begin to write some of his own messages. Again the teacher avoids pressure. She helps whenever help is needed. She praises what comes out right. She overlooks much that is inaccurate. Above all, her aim is to have children who *want* to write. Why?

Writing is complementary to reading. In reading one is trying to extract someone else's message; in writing one is sending one's own message to another person. In reading we take the meaning out of sentences, phrases and words; in writing we build up the message from letters into words, into sentences. What the child learns in writing is of great use to him in reading. So, before the child can 'really read' his first book he will probably be asking you to help him to write letters and words. You should respond to his requests, and, like the teacher, be his scribe, or secretary.

But keep it simple.

## How do children ever learn to read without learning their letters, or sounds, first?

Most reading specialists believe that it is important for the reader to think about 'the message' from the beginning. Before they make any real progress, children have to know that reading *means* 'getting the message'. This is why teachers arrange for them to experience the process at a very early stage through using the simple little pre-primer books we have described. As soon as they have this feeling for the task in hand, the teacher will start directing their attention to letters, sounds, and parts of words. Before long, 'real reading books' will extend their experience of the way these units work together to produce messages which can be understood.

Over the next few years, most children will build up vast experience of letter-sound relationships, and the patterns of language written down.

Learning to read is planned to be an interesting and satisfying experience. The idea is to have the material full of meaning from the start so that children are stimulated to think about what they are reading. This is not pampering children. It is not sugar-coating the pill. It is merely making sensible use of what is known about the process of learning to read.

And, of course, in the writing they are doing, children are working with letters and the true sounds of language all the time. If you like to put it that way, they are using phonics from the very beginning. They are finding ways to represent the sounds they can hear, in print.

## Should parents blame the school if their children have real problems with reading?

Some teachers are of course more capable than others, and there are difficult classes. If you feel particularly dissatisfied with the education your child is receiving there are steps that you should feel able to take, like seeking a second and independent opinion, firstly within the school, from the Principal. The school should have considerable resources to bring to your child's problem, and the way you approach the school should help to gain access to these resources.

If this proves unsatisfactory, there may be a reading teacher with special training or a psychologist who could take an independent view of your child's progress.

However, before blaming the school there are several things that should be thought about.

Schools usually receive children six years after birth. Scientists know, without a doubt, that these early years are extremely important for learning and the development of intelligence.

Well-prepared children seldom fail to learn to read but 'ill-equipped' children tend to go from bad to worse. Handicapped, they fall behind. Then, because they can't read, they become disheartened and stop trying.

All families have their 'ups and downs' and these commonly affect the children's lives and may impede progress or even bring about regression. On the other hand, a 'good year' for the family often means excellent progress for the child, sometimes despite the school.

When you relocate you change many of the secure things in your six-year-old's life. The child has to face a completely different set of school people and different teacher demands. Some take it in their stride. Others take time.

Schools are not able to provide teaching on a one-to-one basis. Try to imagine that you are a teacher with thirty children in your class, all with different needs, at different levels, with different temperaments, some with unhelpful homes and a few with physical and emotional problems. Individual help is obviously not possible for all children all the time. Most learning has to be in a group situation.

As we said earlier, well-prepared children seldom fail to learn to read and it is in the preschool years that we have the opportunity to prepare our children by providing informal one-to-one learning situations in everyday life where the child learns language, and learns how to learn. These experiences prepare him for further learning in a group at school.

To end this chapter on a cheerful note and to illustrate what we mean by a child who has discovered how to learn from experience we would like to quote the following anecdote, supplied by Yetta Goodman who, like her husband Kenneth Goodman, is a leading authority on the reading process.

We were sitting in an airport and a little four-year-old came over to me and she was one of these kids who tells her life story in five minutes. I knew about her mother and her father, and he's gone off somewhere, and then all of a sudden she said to me, 'You know I can read.' And I said, 'Oh really?' She said 'Yes'. So I said, 'What can you read?' She backed up, and I was sitting underneath a little overhang so I couldn't see what she was looking at. She said, 'I can read "taxi"'. And I said, 'Oh really? How do you know?' And she said, 'Because it says T.R.A.N.S.P.O.R.T.A.T.I.O.N.'

Those things are happening to me over and over again with 2, 3, and 4-year-olds. They're aware that there's something being said there but they don't have the relationship with the alphabetic, they have the relationship of the idea.

# 6 Books for parents and children

We have included this section as a chapter to emphasize its importance. All too often 'bibliographies' or 'booklists' are overlooked or ignored.

## Books for parents

We feel that this list, which we have purposely kept short, will help you to stay interested and involved in your child's learning life.

There are many experiences that your child needs in the preschool years to make him or her an avid reader when he or she is older. We have not stressed books on the *teaching* of reading but rather we have selected books which will help parents to provide experiences that their children will certainly need if they are to become good readers.

All books described are straightforward, readable and, at the time of writing, in print. This means that any good bookstore should be able to obtain them if asked. You would also expect to find most of them in libraries.

We have intentionally avoided recommending heavy, 'scholarly' books, no matter how good. Parents are busy people who are likely to be tired when they come home from work. Nor have we quoted prices. These change from time to time, but a bookstore should be able to give you current information.

If you have any difficulty buying or borrowing any title, ask your public library to get it in for you. Librarians are usually pleased to have borrowers use the services they provide.

Every book on this list could give you pleasure, information and, we hope, inspiration. Try them.

*Babies Need Books*, by Dorothy Butler (Atheneum). This book is written for parents who enjoy *Reading Begins At Home*. The author did not like having to make a short list for *Reading Begins At Home* and has produced over 400 suggestions for parents in this later book.

*A Parent's Guide to Children's Reading*, by Nancy Larrick (Doubleday). This book is a classic in the field but parents would be wise to seek the most recent edition because they will want to get to the most recent publications for children.

*How Children Learn*, by John Holt (Dell). This is a chatty book, full of anecdotes. It begins, 'I am sitting on a friend's terrace. Close by is Lisa, 16 months old...' Holt writes in such a personal way that you are impelled to keep reading. He says that his book is 'more about children than about child psychology' and hopes that people who read it 'will come to feel, or feel more than when they opened it, that children are interesting and worth looking at'. The chapter called 'Reading' has some fascinating insights. This is a fundamental book, about children and adults as they really are.

*Focus on Meaning: Talking to some purpose with young children*, by Joan Tough (Allen & Unwin). There are ways of talking to and with young children which help to increase their understanding and fluency. The art is not difficult to learn, once the process is understood, and Dr. Tough's suggestions are very easy to follow. She gives examples of adults and children talking together, and analyses the way in which learning occurs. It all makes fascinating reading; you'll find yourself really *listening* to your children, and devising your own methods for improving communication in the family.

*Learning Through Play*, by Jean Marzollo and Janice Lloyd (Harper & Row). An irresistible little volume which looks almost like a book of cartoons (the kids will love it!). The authors direct their book at people who enjoy children 'and marvel at the ways they grow physically, emotionally and intellectually'. They say 'the emphasis is on learning, particularly at home'. Each double spread covers at least one and sometimes two topics, games or activities. Hilarious line illustrations abound. A real manual, you'll wear it out before the children go to school!

*How To Play With Your Children (And When Not To)*, by Brian & Shirley Sutton-Smith (Dutton). This is a unique book. No other title available covers such a wide range or deals with the educational and emotional value of play in quite the same way. The Sutton-Smiths have five children, and have used their own experiences in writing. They believe firmly in getting in touch and staying in touch and describe with great good humor and in some detail how this can be accomplished. Instructions, suggestions and explanations cover gradual steps. A quote to inspire you! '...your best answer to the future of civilization

might be on the floor — flat on your back, holding up your one-year-old baby, and making faces at each other'. A true handbook, to keep and use.

There are many more books available, but those listed above will provide a place to start. You can face your children's childhood with confidence and the expectation of fun. And experience proves that parental help works *only* if it can be fun, for both parties. Children need to be enjoyed if they are to become enjoying people. And surely, this is what we want for them, before all else?

## Books for children
The following lists of books for reading aloud are intended as guides only. Many, many suitable books

are available. Library borrowing will augment home ownership, provide hints for buying, and introduce children to a very good habit.

For babies, from birth to about eighteen months, begin with 'naming' books. These show a clear, uncluttered picture at each opening. Often, they have a single word or sentence to each picture. Many are either alphabet or number books. For example:

*B is for Bear*, by Dick Bruna (Methuen)
*Story to Tell*, by Dick Bruna (Methuen)
*Goodnight Moon*, by Margaret W. Brown (Harper & Row)

A nursery rhyme collection acquired at this stage will give years of service. Choose from dozens of versions, at a wide range of prices. Your enthusiasm in using the rhymes is more important than the actual volume — but you will enjoy a beautiful book as much as your child. Examples are:

*The Mother Goose Treasury*, by Raymond Briggs (Dell)
*Mother Goose*, by Brian Wildsmith (Merrimack Book Service)
*The Real Mother Goose*, by Blanche Wright (Rand)

Now is also the time to start using finger plays and traditional 'jingles'. The following inexpensive little books will fill most of your needs:

>*Finger Rhymes*, collected and illustrated by Marc
>    Brown (Dutton)
>*Father Fox's Penny Rhymes*, by Clyde Watson
>    (Scholastic Book Service)

From eighteen months to two and a half years, continue with nursery rhymes and established favorites, adding very simple stories such as:

*Rosie's Walk*, by Pat Hutchins (Macmillan)
*But Where is the Green Parrot?* by Thomas and
    Wanda Zacharios (Delacorte)
*Who Took the Farmer's Hat?* by Joan Nodset and
    Fritz Siebel (Scholastic Book Service)
*The Snowy Day*, by Ezra Keats (Viking)

Try different titles from the library. Small children's tastes often surprise their parents!

From two and a half to four years, stories of increasing length and difficulty can be used depending very much on the child, and what has gone before. For example, simple stories such as:

>*Tommy Builds a House* (and other Tommy titles),
>    by Gunilla Wolde (Houghton Mifflin)
>*Harry the Dirty Dog*, by Gene Zion (Harper &
>    Row)
>*Mr. Gumpy's Outing*, by John Burningham
>    (Holt, Rinehart & Winston)
>*The Very Hungry Caterpillar*, by Eric Carle
>    (Philomel)

*Angus and the Ducks*, by Marjorie Flack
    (Doubleday)
*The Box with Red Wheels*, by Maud Petersham
    and Miska Petersham (Macmillan)
*Oh, Lewis!*, by Eve Rice (Penguin)

You could then proceed to longer, slightly more complex stories, like:

>*Blueberries for Sal*, by Robert McCloskey
>    (Penguin)
>*The Cow who Fell in the Canal*, by Phyllis
>    Krasilovsky (Doubleday)
>*The Tale of Peter Rabbit*, by Beatrix Potter
>    (Warne)

Or you could now introduce the 'youngest' of the traditional stories:

>*The Three Bears*, illus. by Paul Galdone
>    (Scholastic Book Service)
>*The Three Little Pigs*, illus. by Paul Galdone
>    (Houghton Mifflin)
>*The Gingerbread Boy*, illus. by Paul Galdone
>    (Houghton Mifflin)
>*The Three Billy Goats Gruff*, illus. by Paul
>    Galdone (Houghton Mifflin)
>*The House that Jack Built*, illus. by Paul Galdone
>    (McGraw Hill)
>*The Old Woman and Her Pig*, illus. by Paul
>    Galdone (McGraw)
>*The Three Bears and 15 Other Stories*, by Anne
>    Rockwell (Harper & Row)

This is also the time when big books about 'things' begin to be treasured, and Richard Scarry enters the scene.

*Richard Scarry's Best Word Book Ever* (Western Publishing Co.)
*Richard Scarry's Hop Aboard, Here We Go* (Western Publishing Co.)
*Fast - Slow, High-Low,* by Peter Spier (Doubleday)
*Truck,* by Donald Crews (Greenwillow)

All of these 'big books' show people and animals involved in every imaginable activity. Children will look at them endlessly, after initial examination with an adult.

From four years on, children's understanding and listening capacity vary widely. This depends on a variety of factors. Most influential perhaps, is previous experience; the 'well-read' four-plus has a large vocabulary and listens with interest and attention. Simple, familiar tales will continue to appeal and may lead on to longer, quite mature stories, such as:

*Mike Mulligan and his Steam Shovel,* by Virginia Lee Burton (Houghton Mifflin)
*Farmer Barnes and the Goats,* by John Cunliffe (Deutsch)
*The Lighthouse Keeper's Lunch,* by Ronda and David Armitage (Deutsch)

*The Camel Who Took a Walk,* Jack Tworkov (Dutton)
*Gilberto and the Wind,* by Marie Ets (Penguin)
*The Curious George series,* by H.E. Rey (Houghton Mifflin)
*The House on East Eighty Eighth Street,* by Bernard Waber (Houghton Mifflin)

By about four years of age, children should be hearing the occasional story *without* (or with few) pictures — perhaps from a collection such as:

*Winnie-the-Pooh,* by A. A. Milne (Dutton)

These pave the way for 'real' reading, when children need to make use of their own imaginations, rather than relying, always, on pictures, however beautiful.

Read these, or other books, to your children daily. Make sure that *your* preschooler is well-prepared for 'real' reading.

## Books mentioned in the text

*Cushla and her Books,* by Dorothy Butler (Horn Books)
*Mike Mulligan and his Steam Shovel,* by Virginia Lee Burton (Houghton Mifflin)
*Young Fluent Readers,* by Margaret Clark (Heinemann Educational)